OYCE GRILL

N CHARACTER

Contents

Art Design: Carmen Fortunato and Jorge Paredes

© 2000 BELWIN-MILLS PUBLISHING CORP. (ASCAP)
All Rights Administered by WARNER BROS. PUBLICATIONS U.S. INC.
All Rights Reserved including Public Performance for Profit

TO THE STUDENT:

The Romantic composers wrote piano pieces called Character Pieces, which expressed the composer's mood or emotion. Each piece was in the "character" of something. A nocturne, for instance, would represent something about night. After you have learned a piece, give it a "picture title" that represents your mood or emotion as you play the piece.

bagatelle: a trifle
barcarolle: a boat song suggesting a rocking motion
nocturne: about night
prelude: a piece based on one idea

TO THE TEACHER:

These pieces contain rhythmic, melodic and harmonic patterns that occur in the Romantic works. *Fingering is very important. Students should change the fingering to fit their hands.* Be sure to have them write in the new fingerings.

Although some pedaling is indicated, the ear should be the judge.

Joyce Grill

PRELUDE

E minor

JOYCE GRILL

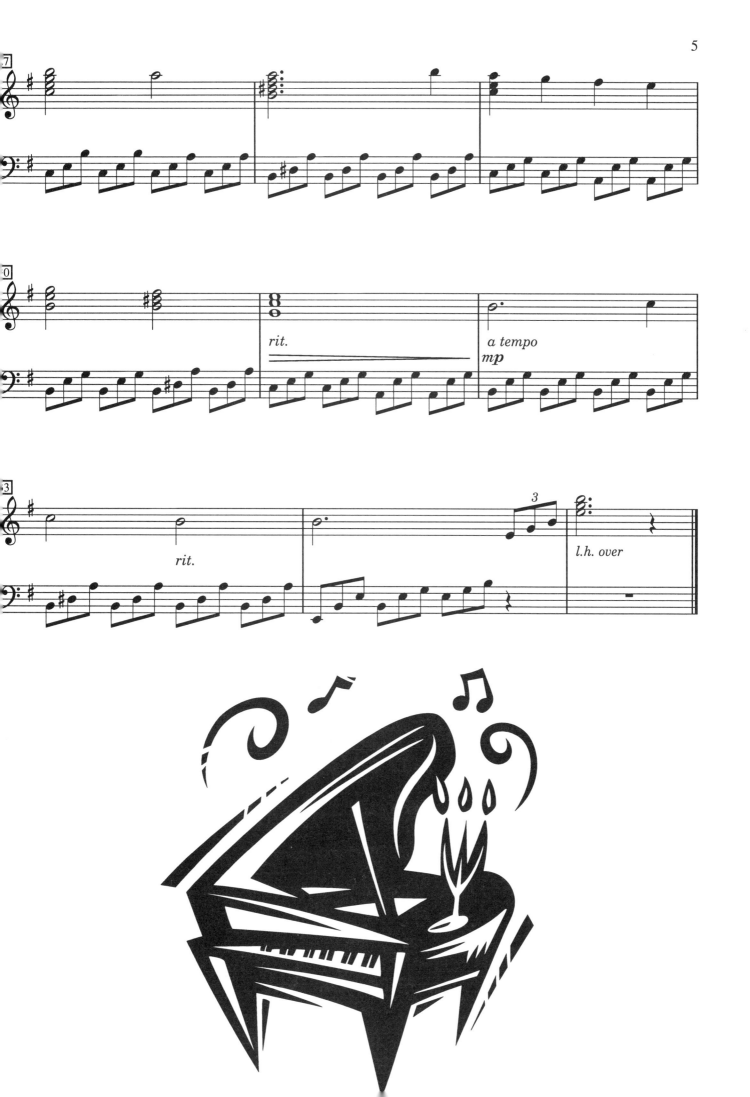

BAGATELLE

D minor

JOYCE GRIL

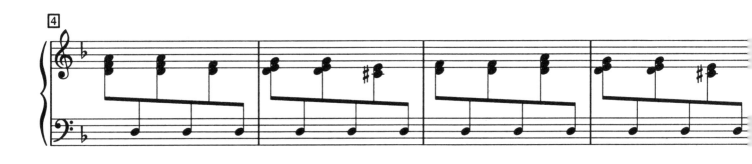

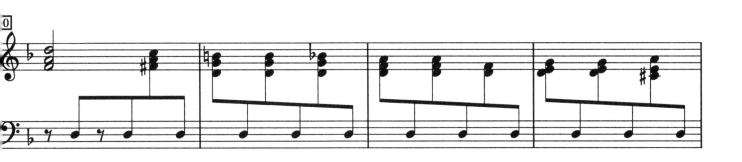

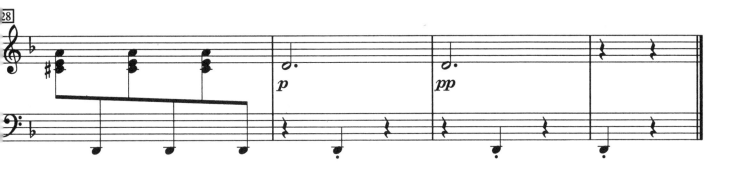

NOCTURNE

G major

JOYCE GRIL

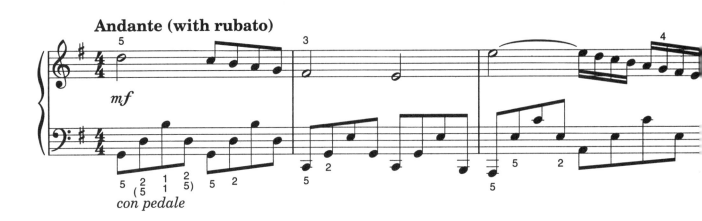

BAGATELLE

G major

JOYCE GRILL

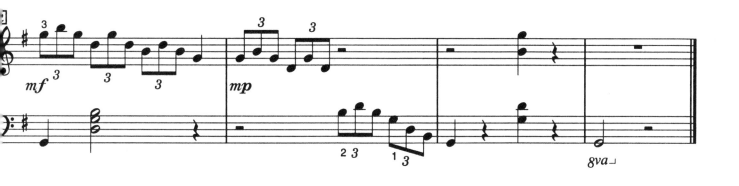

PRELUDE

F major

JOYCE GRILL

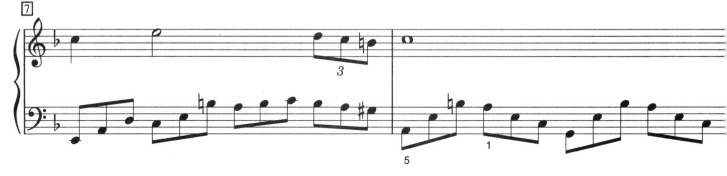

half ped. to the end

8va⌐

BARCAROLLE

C minor

JOYCE GRILL

BAGATELLE

C major

JOYCE GRIL

BARCAROLLE

G major

JOYCE GRIL

Joyce Grill

Joyce Grill is in high demand as a piano clinician, focusing on both teacher and student groups. As a former faculty member of the University of Wisconsin–La Cross, Grill has had extensive hands-on teaching experience, which she brings to her clinics. As a result, she conveys not only course-related applications, but also practical and tangible approaches to instruction and student development.

With degrees from the University of Wisconsin–Madison, Grill has had advanced study at the School of Fine Arts in Fontainebleau, France, where she studied with Nadia Boulanger (theory and composition) and with Robert and Jean Casadesus (piano). An active member of MTNA, Grill holds the MTNA Master Teacher Certificate.

Grill founded the La Crosse Area Music Teachers Association. She served as the association's first president and maintains an active role with the organization. She also serves on the boards of the U.S. Music Alumni Association, the La Crosse Public Education foundation, and the Viterbo College Bright Star Series.

Grill is a well-known composer, whose various compositions for Warner Bros. Publications introduce students to the styles of several musical eras. Her original compositions—which are performed throughout the country—have been widely praised by both teachers and students. Grill is a frequent guest conductor for Multi-Piano concerts and is active as a recitalist and accompanist for area faculty recitals and touring professionals.

Piano Music
by Joyce Grill

◆ TEACHING DUETS (one piano, four hands)

A CHRISTMAS MEDLEY
Traditional carols arranged by Joyce Grill
(PA02485) Elementary Level
"Away in a Manger," "Come All Ye Shepherds" and "Silent Night," move easily from carol to carol, resulting in a most sat-isfying performance piece.

GYPSY AIRS
(PA02517) Intermediate Level
With energy, rhythmic excitement, a singing, soaring melody, and great interaction between players, this duet is full of flair and flavor.

JOURNEY OF THE KINGS
Traditional carols arranged by Joyce Grill
(PA02487) Elementary Level
What a journey! This duet keeps moving ahead, sometimes with "March of the Three Kings" and sometimes with "We Three Kings."

O HOLY NIGHT
by Adolphe Adam, arranged by Joyce Grill
(PA02450) Elementary Level
What Christmas joy will be shared through this fine arrangement of a beloved carol! The parts are equally matched.

RING CHRISTMAS BELLS (The Ukranian Carol)
by M. Leontovich, arranged by Joyce Grill
(PA02398) Elementary Level
This duet setting of the happy Ukranian Carol will please both the primo and secondo player; the parts have equal importance.

SONG OF THE WISE MEN
Traditional Puerto Rican carol arranged by Joyce Grill
(PA02451) Elementary Level
This traditional carol of Puerto Rico celebrates the journey of the three wise kings in a very merry way, using a habañera rhythm.

◆ ACCOMPANYING BOOK

THE ACCOMPANIST (Yes, It Really Happened!)
(EL9682)
Joyce Grill knows whereof she speaks. She is a fine accompanist and consequently in great demand. In this little book she recounts some of her experiences on the bench. Its tone is light-hearted, but there are messages. Every musician will identify with the hap-penings. It is a must for every pianist who is expected to "make Genevieve sound great."

◆ SOLO COLLECTIONS

CHARACTER PIECES
(EL03834) Intermediate Level
Character pieces were popular in the Romantic period to "chara ize" a particular mood or idea. Joyce Grill has successfully cre seven pieces that emulate this style.

EITHER/OR
(EL03775) Elementary Level
Broken arm? Sprained finger? Need a change of pace? This book has nine pieces that can be played with either the right or the left hand.

FROM MANY LANDS
(EL03782) Intermediate Level
Created to help students prepare for the Romantic literature, the pieces are based on original folk-like melodies and rhythms, re senting nine countries.

FROM MANY LANDS AT CHRISTMAS
(EL9592) Intermediate Level
With eleven Christmas songs and carols from eleven countries, is a diversity of styles and sounds.

JUST FOR FUN!
(EL03939) Intermediate Level
Students will have fun making good music. Each of the seven piece a jazzy feel. Rhythms are easy to read and feel, with appealing titles

LEFT ALONE — RIGHT ON!
(EL9503) Intermediate Level
MORE LEFT ALONE — RIGHT ON!
(EL9695) Intermediate Level
Each piece is written for left hand alone or for right hand alone, is structured on a specfic musical concept. Providing great sight r ing material for more advanced students and excellent transiti material for transfer students.

PRELUDES
(EL9718) Intermediate Level
Ten original pieces in the Romantic style, calling for diffe approaches and attitudes by the performer. Most of the prel sound much harder than they really are!

◆ TEACHING SOLOS

THE BLACK CAT BOOGIES
(PA02427) Elementary Level

THANKS, ANNA MAGDALENA (Minuet Boogie)
(PA02465) Intermediate Level

ner Bros. Publications proudly presents two superb series of books that contain works by the master composers of each period. The selections within each book are arranged in a progressive order of difficulty.

Each book features:

- A preface describing the musical styles relating to the economy, culture, fashion, and art of the times.
- Beautiful cover art.
- Careful editing for the correct performance, with fingerings and written-out ornaments.
- Various composers representing several countries and musical styles.

E PIANO MASTERS SERIES

nal Piano Solos by Master Composers of the Period
Compiled and Edited by Dale Tucker

THE BAROQUE MASTERS
(EL96114) Upper Intermediate
11 titles: Prelude in D Minor, Prelude No. 1 in C Major and Two-Part Inven-tion No. 8 in F Major (J.S. Bach) • Allemande and Prelude No. 8 in E Minor (Couperin) • Sarabande in F Major (Handel) • La Joyeuse
u) • Sonata in C Major and Sonata in D Minor (Scarlatti) • e in F Major and Fantasia in C Minor (Telemann).

THE CLASSICAL MASTERS
(EL96115) Upper Intermediate
9 titles: Für Elise, Minuet in G Major and Sonatina in G Major/First Movement (Beethoven) • Sonatina op. 36, no. 1/First Movement (Clementi) • Finale from Sonata No. 43 (Haydn) • Six Variations in G and Vivace from Sonata op. 55, no. 1 (Kuhlau) • Finale from Sonatina No. 6 and Rondo from Sonata K. 545 (Mozart).

THE ROMANTIC MASTERS
(EL96116) Upper Intermediate
16 titles: Arabesque op. 100, no. 2 and Ballade op. 100, no. 15 (Burgmüller) • Prelude op. 28, no. 4 and Prelude op. 29, no. 7 (Chopin) • Spinning Song (Ellmenreich) • Patriotic Song (Grieg)
ning Song and Scherzo (Gurlitt) • To a Wild Rose
owell) • Ecossaise in D Major (Schubert), Berceuse op. 124,
The Happy Farmer and The Wild Horseman (Schumann) •
Song, Morning Prayer and The Sick Doll (Tchaikovsky).

THE CONTEMPORARY MASTERS
(EL96117) Upper Intermediate
14 titles: Allegro and Bagatelle op. 6, no. 6 (Bartók) • Le Petite Berger and Le Petite Nègre (Debussy) • Prelude No. 2 (Gershwin) • Waltz op. 123, no. 6) (Gretchaninoff) • Playing Ball and Toccatina op. 27, no. 6 (Kabalevsky) • The Bagpipes, Lullaby and The Manger (Menotti), Gymnopedie No. 1 (Satie) • The Mechanical
hostakovitch) • Vivo (Stravinsky).

EASY SOLOS BY THE MASTERS SERIES

Original Piano Solos by Master Composers of the Period
Compiled and Edited by Dale Tucker

EASY SOLOS BY THE BAROQUE MASTERS
(EL9702) Easy/Intermediate

17 titles: Chorale in F Major, Minuet in G Major, Musette in D Major and Polonaise in G Minor (Bach) • King William's March and Trumpet Minuet (Clarke) • Le Petite Rein (Couperin) • Bourée No. 1 in G Major and Sarabande in D Minor (Handel) • Air in D Minor (Purcell) • Rondino in C Major (Rameau) and more.

EASY SOLOS BY THE CLASSICAL MASTERS
(EL9703) Easy/Intermediate

17 titles: Country Dance in D Major and Ecossaise in G Major (Beethoven) • Morning (Diabelli) • Air and Variations in A Major, Allegretto in G Major, German Dance in D Major and Quadrille (Haydn) • Allegro in B-flat Major and Minuet in G Major (Mozart) • Little Dance and Youthful Joy (Türk) and others.

EASY SOLOS BY THE ROMANTIC MASTERS
(EL9704) Easy/Intermediate

15 titles: Sonatina in C Major (Biehl) • Andante in F Major, Bright Is the Sky, The Festive Dance and In the Garden (Gurlitt) • Children's Song (Kohler) • Ecossaise in G Major (Schubert) • Melody op. 68, no. 1 and Soldier's March op. 68, no. 2 (Schumann) • Old French Song op. 39, no. 6 (Tchaikovsky) and more.

EASY SOLOS BY THE CONTEMPORARY MASTERS
(EL9705) Easy/Intermediate

13 titles: Dance in C Major and Song of the Vagabond (Bartók) • Peasant Dance (Goedicke) • The Little Beggar (Gretchaninoff) • Dance in F Major and Theme and Variations (Kabalevsky) • The Bear (Rebikov) • Berceuse (Satie) • Soldier's March (Shostakovitch) • Andantino in C Major (Stravinsky) and others.